7·99

Dancing In The Street
& 9 more motown greats

CONTENTS

Ain't No Mountain High Enough	Diana Ross	2
Dancing In The Street	Martha Reeves and the Vandellas	5
I Heard It Through The Grapevine	Gladys Knight and the Pips/ Marvin Gaye	8
I Want You Back	Jackson Five	16
I'm Still Waiting	Diana Ross	11
My Guy	Mary Wells	23
Papa Was A Rollin' Stone	Temptations	31
Reach Out I'll Be There	Four Tops	20
Stop! In The Name Of Love	Supremes	26
You Are The Sunshine Of My Life	Stevie Wonder	34

Production: Miranda Steel

Cover photographs supplied by Redferns

Published 1999

International Music Publications

International Music Publications Limited
Griffin House 161 Hammersmith Road London W6 8BS England

DON'T BE A MUSIC COPYCAT!

The copying of © copyright material is a criminal offence and may lead to prosecution

Reproducing this music in any form is illegal and forbidden by the Copyright, Designs and Patents Act, 1988

Ain't No Mountain High Enough

Words and Music by
NICKOLAS ASHFORD and VALERIE SIMPSON

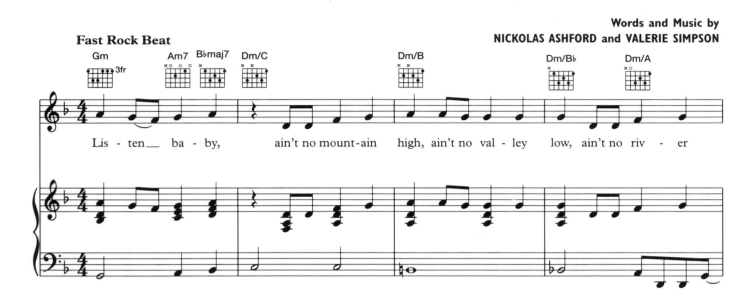

© 1967 Jobete Music Co Inc, USA
Jobete Music Co Inc/EMI Music Publishing Ltd, London WC2H 0EA

2 I set you free
I told you you could always count on me
From that day on, I made a vow
I'll be there when you want me
Some way, some how
'Cause baby there (Chorus)

3 My love is alive
Way down in my heart
Although we are miles apart
If you ever need a helping hand
I'll be there on the double
As fast as I can
Don't you know that there (Chorus)

Dancing In The Street

Words and Music by
IVY JO HUNTER, WILLIAM STEVENSON and MARVIN GAYE

Call - ing out a - round the world, are you rea - dy for a brand new beat?
in - vi - ta - tion a - cross the na - tion, a chance for folks to meet.

Sum - mer's here and the time is right for danc - ing in the street.
There'll be laugh - ing, sing - ing and mu - sic swing - ing danc - ing in the street.

They're danc - ing in Chi - ca - go, down in New Or - leans,
Phil - a - del - phia, P. A., Bal - ti - more and D. C. Now

© 1964 Jobete Music Co Inc and Stone Agate Music, USA
Jobete Music Co Inc/EMI Music Publishing Ltd, London WC2H 0EA

3 People say believe half what you see
   Son, and none of what you hear
   But I can't help bein' confused
   If it's true please tell me dear
   Do you plan to let me go
   For the other guy you loved before?

I'm Still Waiting

Words and Music by
DEKE RICHARDS

© 1970 Jobete Music Co Inc, USA
Jobete Music Co Inc/EMI Music Publishing Ltd, London WC2H 0EA

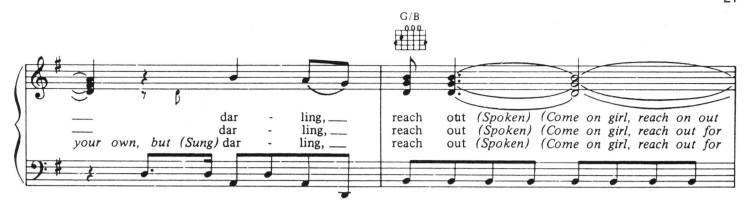
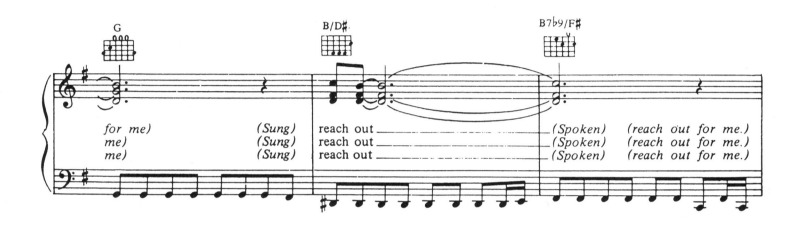

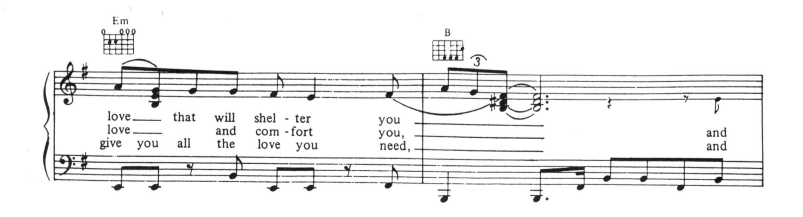

Stop! In The Name Of Love

Words and Music by
BRIAN HOLLAND, LAMONT DOZIER and EDDIE HOLLAND

© 1965 Stone Agate Music, USA
Jobete Music Co Inc/EMI Music Publishing Ltd, London WC2H 0EA

Papa Was A Rollin' Stone

Words and Music by
NORMAN WHITFIELD and BARRETT STRONG

© 1972 Stone Diamond Music Corp, USA
Jobete Music Co Inc/EMI Music Publishing Ltd, London WC2H 0EA

2 Hey, Mama, I heard Papa call himself a jack of all trades
Tell me, is that what sent Papa to an early grave
Folks say Papa would beg, borrow or steal to pay his bills
Hey, Mama, folks say Papa was never much on thinkin'
Spend most of his time chasin' women and drinkin'
Mama, I'm depending on you to tell me the truth
(Spoken:) Mama just hung her head and said, 'Son,...
(To Chorus)